Praise

"If I love you, will I lose myself?"
speaks to the underlying theme of Closer
to Closure. Drew Walker's poetry is
steeped with rhyme and meter, the spoken
word of love-seeking and love-lost,
"a stirring ache" in this "beautiful
tragedy."

— Laurie Lynn Muirhead,
author of Coyote Snow

In a time when writers' creativity and
craft is undermined and threatened by AI,
Drew Walker's reflective and unique book
reminds us of the importance of human
emotion and nature's inspiration. As
Walker asserts in one of her poems, "Art
is not an afterthought," and poetry is
worthy of its place on these delicate and
beautiful handmade pages.

— Kim Mannix, author of Confirm Humanity

Closer to Closure is a candid, clever, and
grounding read, not unlike the presence
of the author herself. Recommended for
anyone who understands that trees are
cool in every sense of the word or simply
has an appreciation for the fullness of
the human experience, and the beautiful
pages that hold them.

— Joy Love, Poet

Drew Walker offers you a glimpse into the world of love, loss, mistakes, fears, and a constant struggle to find and love oneself. She expresses her emotions through concise language. She uses a pittance of words to express regret and vulnerability, anguish and ecstasy, love and loss. Bold colours and texture you swear you can smell and taste as she utters "when everything becomes too much, that's when you're supposed to cry."

- Daniel Poitras,
poet in Beaver Hills House

The spirit of humanity throbs through these pages. Listening to undeniable universal truths being captured by these pages. Moved and heard and listened to by these pages. Leaves one feeling stood with in a solidarity of the spirit. Closer to Closure cloaks your heart in warmth and understanding.

- Ryan James Summers aka Some-Sum;
poet, host, emcee, story teller,
artist

Published 2025
Printed in Canada

ISBN Print 978-1-997770-03-9
ISBN Ebook 978-1-997770-04-6

Cover Design by Drew Walker & Alexis Marie Chute
Interior typewritten pages by Drew Walker

For information address:
Wild Skies Press
A division of Alexis Marie Productions Inc.
Edmonton, Alberta, Canada
info@alexismariechute.com
www.WildSkiesPress.com

Wild Skies Press is an independent literary publisher
founded in 2021. Wild Skies refers to the Aurora
Borealis-northern lights-in Alberta, where the press is
located, situated on Treaty 6 Territory. Wild Skies Press
publishes non-fiction, fiction, poetry, and hybrid genres
with an emphasis on the creation of Canadian works and
books by emerging and established authors.
www.WildSkiesPress.com

Closer to Closure

Preface:

The following poems were written
by Drew Walker between 2020-2024
while residing in Canada. At this
time in her life, she was coming
home after several years of solo
travel abroad, navigating relationships
both ending and beginning. The words
in this book coincide with international
heartbreak, long distance love, deep
friendship, the struggle of settling
down, and the pursuit of presence.

Art is not an afterthought

It is the essence

Of expression
Of creation
Of healing
Of loving
Of living

Drew Walker

In the Bath

Spiraling
Downward, upward, outward,
Inward
Into my mind's eye
Introspecting
Incessant, inspired
In flow, inside
A marriage of sensations
From my hands
And in is out
Outside of my body
Outstanding energy
Out of time
Out of this world
Without seizing
An outro
Spiraling

Drew Walker

Dreams of we
Dreams of two
Dreams of us
Are dreams of you

Drew Walker

Early Spring

Coming out of hibernation

The land is alive

I can hear it breathing

Through the whispers of the treetops

Collectively, it's heart beats

Louder, louder

The louder it gets

The more synchronicities I witness

I can feel my heart beating

With all the other lubs and dubs around me

A moment of ease

Peace in the chaos

As I understand, even if just for a moment

That I am part of something greater

Drew Walker

Death to Love

I can't understand this endless love
A constant state with looming heartache
For those I gave myself to
But who couldn't give in return
It's scary to be so open
To love, to loss, to life
I have this unjustified fear of stagnation
That no one will live up to my expectation
I need to be free
With or without, no hard feelings
I'm afraid of this collection
Of hearts unhealed
Did I break them?
Did I trap them? Like caged animals
Wounded as I nurture them
Where death is more humane
But what if they fully recover?
Would I then reap rewards for my care?
Or is it that I can't handle death?
Death to the past
Death to myself
Death to love

Drew Walker

Artistry

I feel we're connected
In a way that is poetic
In the way we choose to live our lives
Creating stories as time flies
How we're both seeking inspiration
Fighting back against stagnation
Creating art from all we see
Traveller's treat; this one's on me
Our lives collided when it was right
The path is winding, you're always a light
I wonder if we'll have a chance
Under the stars, we can dance
Sharing songs and poems of the beauty in our heart
Realizing it is life itself that is the work of art

Drew Walker

Delayed Gratification

There is so much to learn
From observing the land
I'm amazed at industrial detachment:
Building extravagant structures
Inevitably temporary
Eager to inhabit carcasses
So much so
That care is absent

Imagine a layout
That works with nature
Creating, lasting
Impermanent in design
As it evolves
Do it once
Do it right
We make too much work
But there's more we can make

How strange it is
To perceive more ease
In opposition to our Mother

Drew Walker

Snuggletown

No stress, no worries, all love
I'm glad you visited that night
With a message to deliver
Then we met in real life

I think that we are soul mates
Diving face first down the slide
How can this be possible:
Two hearts to just collide?

There's a knowing in each other
That now is not our time
But it's the ultimate temptation
When the neighbour gives us wine

When I'm looking at your face
I see your hairs turn grey
A sign of all your chapters
Through your growth and your decay

In each other's presence
We are free from all disguise
Surrendered in your arms
I see forever in your eyes

                    Drew Walker

I'm letting go of desire.
For each time I long for something,
It takes me further from where I am.
I am here. I am now. I am.

Drew Walker

Flight Home

I've seen this all before
But how many times will it pass my eyes
Will it pass through my body
Until I've received what I'm supposed
    to be learning?
The themes of my life
Will repeat again and again
If something does not change within me.
So I will run, what a surprise.
But this time, back to the place I've abandoned.
Will it be different this time?
I have changed, I can feel it.
I can feel everything.
Imagine being attached to a person so sensitive
    that they can feel things unlike this world.
Unless you feel it, it's impossible to describe.
But once you feel it, it can never be unfelt.
Tell me you wouldn't feel different after that,
    tell me you'd never change.
Even if you told me so,
I wouldn't believe you
It must've been a different feeling.
I won't run, no.
It's too fast these days.
But I'll walk.

                    Drew Walker

I can only be the one for one.

The one I choose is myself

Drew Walker

I won't mistake this loneliness for loving you

I won't mistake this loneliness for loving you

I won't mistake this loneliness for loving you

I won't mistake this loneliness for loving you

I won't mistake this loneliness for loving you

I won't mistake this loneliness for loving you

I won't mistake this loneliness for loving you

I won't mistake this loneliness for loving you

I won't mistake this loneliness for loving you

Drew Walker

There's a difference between

wanting to do something

and

being capable of doing something

Drew Walker

I thought I could fix you

But here I am,

broken

Drew Walker

Wedding Vows

Today is the day
I would have thee wed
Given you my hand
Been a wife in your bed
An interesting change
From what I expected
We couldn't eb with the flow
And became all too hectic
Instead I take my hand
And on this day I vow
To not get so lost in the future
That I lose sight of now
I vow to respect my own self
And to set boundaries
To keep my heart open
And feel everything with ease
To trust that little voice
Inside of my head
That's speaking the truth
And guiding my tread
I vow to always listen
To what my body is feeling
To the centres that cry
For reflection and healing
To take things even slower
When my instinct is to jump
To notice patterns from the past
That have resulted in a slump
I vow to love myself so deeply
And love everything around
To keep in touch with my emotions
Balance all that is found

I vow to forgive every pain
And any person I may blame
I want to heal every pattern
Creating cycles of shame
I will try to accept what is
And what will be
I vow to let the **things** unfold
The way that things will want to be
This is the marriage of my heart
To my heart as it is true
'Til death do us part
I vow always: I do

Drew Walker

Strength and Flexibility

How can I live
         in a world that's so wrong?

This thought has been nurtured
         for far too long

Everyday ruminating
         on problems I see

Overlooking simple beauties
         within reality

Many of these moments
         some to come and some have gone

Are the spiral of life
         in action all along

I will consciously reframe
         and live positively

Aligning higher wisdom
         and divinity

                    Drew Walker

Capricorn Skies

I'm trying not to think of you
Out of fear that you will change
If I retrieve the memories
Will you remain the same?

Or will I make a hero
Through my glorified lens
When the time is right to reunite
My ideas are all pretend

Still I can't stop thinking
You're all that's on my mind
This feeling of alrightness
And knowing you're my kind

Do you ever think of me?
About that comfort in my eyes
Distant love, you're taking over
Under Capricorn skies

Drew Walker

Healing

Standstill
A frozen evolution
Triggered stagnation
Unmoving surround
The only way out
Is in
Deep into
Find the root
Face it
Look at it
Straight in the eyes
Forgive it
Accept it
Release it
Release yourself
Realize yourself
Realize your potential
Redefine
Real life

Drew Walker

First Date

I feel it in my heart
Pounding
Overflowing
A slow breath isn't enough
to control the flutter
Am I ready to do this all again?
Can I stand to let another in?
How cruel it would be to deny myself
To close myself
To bring the past into the present
It would punish us both
Already I'm alarmed
Of the synchronicities at hand
So I'm approaching with caution
As we dive on in

Drew Walker

Flight

I'm sorry that I left in the way I did
I didn't have the strength to explain
Our love was overpowering
And it left me with great pain

I never intended to turn away
From what I saw as lasting love
My fears and doubts fed negatively
I couldn't get back to what was

You gave me a home and your family
I felt welcomed with open hearts
You taught me about the depths of the world
I still can't believe we're apart

My heart feels heavy when you cross my mind
I just want to know you're alright
I carry our love, endlessly
Even though I left on that flight

Drew Walker

Blood

Residual smoke flowing into my lungs
I forget why I'm really here
That quality time we so desperately seek
But I can't feel the love when I'm near

It seems that we're stuck in our heads these days
Our identities attached to the thoughts
Bury the shadows at the end of your glass
Reality is ridden with knots

I fear for our future, imbalance persists
Physical suffering when presence resists
Our time is impermanent, you already know this
I'll search for forever, together in bliss

Drew Walker

I can accept you

And I can accept me

But I can't accept us

Drew Walker

Thinking

Sometimes I'm afraid
    to put my pen to paper
If I don't know my true feelings
    maybe then it would be easier
If I let them live inside,
    maybe then they'd change
And when I put the pen to paper,
    my thoughts are rearranged

But the longer they're inside,
    the harder they are to find
I'm convinced of all these lies
    as they are buried in my mind
The truth can break the strife
    but I'm not one for closing doors
There's impermanence to life
    and you can't live here anymore

Drew Walker

The you I knew was a beautiful person
How sad
That you could never see yourself
    the way I knew you to be

                    Drew Walker

Answered Question

What could it be that I'm looking for?
In a lover, a partner, one to open the door
Who talks and listens,
        picks me up from the floor
One to build my understanding more and more

Being silly is the key to lasting love, I'm sure
When life gets too serious, laughter is the cure
When the other needs a hug
        it takes one look, a lure
A shared contemplation
        on the things we will endure

I want to realize my potential
        in the experience of love
Be uplifted and empowered
        to kiss the stars above
Trusting in my own judgements
        and decisions thereof
Without fear of any guilt
        because our minds fit like a glove

I plan to go through life
        with all its ebbs and all its flows
I realize that the highs
        mean nothing without the lows
I will embrace my nature and connections;
        it'll take me where it goes
Through all the peaks and all the valleys;
        where it goes, no one knows

Drew Walker

This Lady

I can't stop looking at this woman
Radiating femininity through the layers of her skin
When she looks me in the eyes,
I feel her seeing me
When I whisper in her ear
I feel her hearing me
When her hand caresses mine,
I feel her touching me
She knows my thoughts before I think them
My dreams before I dream them
She tucks me in before I'm sleeping
And feeds me breakfast in the morning
This lady is the one for me
This lady in the mirror I see

Drew Walker

Enamor

Love
That indescribable feeling
The one that a poet
Will spend a lifetime
In search of words for
My heart is feeling again
It's grown in size I'm sure
Based on the way my breath has changed
I don't know if there's an Earthly way
To release these feelings
Imagine the possibility
Of two becoming one
And staying one
A fusion of senses
As if walking through a person
To truly know and be a person
A collision of lives
Creating a shared reality
An unfleeting connection
That overwhelms emotional capacity
As it deepends over time
To depths undiscovered

Drew Walker

The state of your physical world

Is a reflection of your state of mind

Drew Walker

Entangled Memories

I feel like reaching out
To let you know that there are times
When I just miss you
I want to be held
And I flashback to our companionship
How we really just rode a wave together
In pursuit of pleasure
Loving, learning, exploring, feeling
Planning - for something else
Something to get us out of our current entanglement
Every time you visit my mind
I am met with an intense sensation in my chest
It is heavy and it is open
It can still feel the intensity of our love
But still feels the lasting ripple of the end
In those moments, I sit in my missing you
I feel it deeply
And I keep moving on

Drew Walker

San Marcos La Laguna

The warm breeze caresses my skin
I am being seduced
Pure sensuality awakens my body
My spirit is nature's muse
It tickles my toes
And kisses my cheek
Takes a piece of my aura
It's hers to keep
My body is open
My soul is healing
Met again as I find
The next level of feeling

Drew Walker

Healthy Hesitation

This isn't the first time
    that I've been told

By a lover with me
    that he wants to grow old

That I'm beautiful, smart,
    when you know you know

That I'll be a great mother,
    we'll continue to grow

It feels a little different
    each time around

This time feels real
    and my feet are on the ground

A true sense of home
    is all that I've been seeking

Like the one in your arms
    and the words we've been speaking

I'm filled with gratitude for us
    and the pace that we go

Some say tap the brakes
    but for us we're moving slow

It's for you and I to decide
    special moments of glory

And when to share it with the world
    as we write our love story

Drew Walker

Gardener's Poem

Planting little seeds of change
While moving upwards in life
A person has only so much space in the garden
What do I want to reach maturity?
I must keep in mind what requires more water,
What produces most yield,
            what could possibly take over
Think about how all these plants go to seed
Cycling through, I'll continue to feed
While I make this decision
I also choose which to pluck
The seedlings that won't serve me
No longer tend to, out of luck
But even seeds that are discarded
Can sometimes reappear
Sparking joy in your garden
Pushing through, they volunteer
Just as we nurture our gardens
We must also nurture our thoughts
Nature feeds unto itself
What will you plant across?

                    Drew Walker

Tax Time

Why is our collective default
              to complicate

To make distant worlds removed
                from our real state

To discipline morality and punish
              those who educate

To nurture sick societies in hopes
              they will reciprocate

Drew Walker

Heat

I want to dig into your skin
You've taken control, I grab ahold
Throw me around
Do whatever you want
Pure desire
Feeling your breath on my neck
Moving further from my eyes
This must be wrong
But we know it's right
The spark ignites
Blood pulsing
Long in the making
And we've finally broken down
We can't take it any longer
Excitement growing stronger
Tie me even tighter
Or untie me entirely
Take this body and have your way with me
Come away with me

Drew Walker

Rainy Hot Tub

Submerged in amniotic warmth
As cool drops kiss the surface of my face
Body rising, I am covered in kisses
Droplets bouncing off my chest,
                    my abdomen,
                    my thighs
I am comforted by your grasp
Like a welcomed hand to bed
Your kisses do not bounce, but they penetrate
My mind,
my soul,
my love
I pull myself up and the weight of the water
                    guides me back down
A gesture to extend the moment
Grounding my perceptual sensations
As I merge the presence of this body
With the presence of this Earth

                    Drew Walker

More Than Friends

There are so many things
I've been meaning to say
From the day that I met you
I am here to stay
Years are spilling over
And onto this page
You're the music in my heart
I want to share with you my stage

Everything about you
Brings a feeling of alignment
There's freedom in your energy
I hold no fear of confinement
I suppose my only fear
Is that you see me as a friend
That you're not looking for a partner
For a teammate 'til the end

However it unfolds
Is the way it's meant to be
I'll always have you in my heart
And that I hope you see

Drew Walker

We are all reflections of nature

Cycling through our own growth

We pay no mind

    to the changes in the trees

How beautiful it is

    to accept our own changing seasons, too

Drew Walker

Mother's Day Reflections

In my mother's eyes
There's a reflection of myself
A glimpse into the future
Of all emotions felt

This complex experience
Of life as a whole
Is impossible to prepare for
Every choice takes its toll

So many facets
Can't be taught, can't be said
The only way is through feeling
Still it reels in my head

As mother and a child
You are my superwoman
Grown as two adults
I now respect my fellow human

There's only so much
Of this life that we can share
When the time aligns itself
I always love when you are there

This journey holds adversity
And we all will carry pain
Sometimes we put it on each other
But there's nothing here to gain

1/2

When the suffering takes root
It's our responsibility to heal
For it will make us better lovers
With the demons we must deal

I can't yet understand
The way that life has led you here
But I walk along your footprints
Revealing truth to see more clear

I'm ever grateful for your energy
For your guidance and for your wisdom
The cryptic nature of our family
Paves the way to a fruitful kingdom

If you wonder how I feel
Know that love is all I see
I accept you as you are
The only mother for me

Drew Walker

Last Week

When I broke things off
Your request to me
Was to never write
Any poetry
A wish that came
From a place of evil
I told you before:
It's just how I heal
Out of respect
I'll leave you out
Limit my creativity;
Reaffirm my doubt
I'll be careful about
The words I may speak
But I'm feeling better now
Than I did last week

Drew Walker

Fundamental Differences

We all have potential
The ability to grow, climb, evolve
To improve ourselves and the world around us
But we are not our potentials
We are what we are

There is no guarantee of realization
And here I am, yet again
Falling for the potential of who this man could be
And not falling for who he is
We seek to change each other
To better fit the framework of our lives

But the areas of improvement are fundamental
To our differing cognitions
Uncompromising
And yet we say we want to stay,

Commit, build a life, build a family
But buried underneath those words
Is a feeling
Not the feeling of a soulmate
But we don't want to hurt each other
And we don't want to lose love again
And we don't want to be alone
But maybe we have to, and it'll be alright

Drew Walker

Poenetic

Perpetual downfall
A balance to the highs
Grounded, anchored by the weight
Wait, change awaits
In the meantime, mean time
Meaningful in it its own time
Alone time, home time
What is home but a feeling?
Who gives word to the meaning?
Losing sense, a consequence
Mask it with some confidence
I'm confident
In the need to change a scene
See what's in the scene as it needs to be seen
Flip the script, next scene
To a place I've never been
Believe and I will be
New environment, new me

Drew Walker

Family Ties

It's not a lack of love or care
Our blood, connected, everywhere
Some lifestyles don't align with others
Boundaries bound to be discovered
This, too, can change and evolve
Time will tell who to involve
This conversation was bad planning
But it seems we've reached an understanding

Drew Walker

The more you look the more you see

Drew Walker

<u>Little Diddy</u>

When I'm at my best
You're in my mind
Time will tell
What we will find
Crossing oceans
Hearts unwind
Unknown roads
Two of a kind
Distant bodies
Souls aligned
When and where
Can this love bind?
A shining star
Gracefully designed
Give us time
We'll be refined
When feeling low
Let me remind:
One day we'll feel
Our love entwined

Drew Walker

Today is the day

Everyday is the day

Someday will be the day

Another day among the days

Drew Walker

Parallel Universe

Rooted in reality
I am in love
This wondrous life
The place I call home
In my heart and in this space
I am free to flow
In every day and every realm

Another world, a fantasy,
Lingers above
Abundant soils
Crystal ley lines
A calling to behold
Second life
Second love
My spirit awaits
A mere contemplation
Of an unreachable place

Drew Walker

Christmas Market

Bottle up this feeling

A magical dreaming

Tickled by the twinkling night

Warmth by the fire light

Sweetness running through my bones

Chocolate insulation, a taste of home

Smiles natural, ear to ear

Ease of being with sisters near

A joyful season of holiday cheer

Time well spent, hearts sincere

Drew Walker

8 Abbotsfield

Another day on public transit
Here I'm with the general public
A diverse range, this city's cast
Seeing people from my past
The seats here smell like sweat and smoke
Behind the driver, have a toke
Open a window, get some air
There's stories within every chair
Every stain and every scratch
Upholstery doesn't even match
Absent eyes and people dark
At least I won't have to pay to park

Drew Walker

Lovestruck

Words are completely failing me
All of my surrounds: seemingly insignificant
I am irreparably addicted
To everything about you
To every single part of you
To all that is surrounding you
This heart of mine belongs to you

Drew Walker

Work Mode

Tell me where the time's gone
For I've lost all sense
Busy overstimulation
Distracted, disconnected hence

How is time so
That it passes me by
But when I'm taking life slow
I never wonder why?

The city noise masks my dissociation
A churning inside; bubbbling frustration
Magnified are the patterns of societal stagnation
That I feed into everyday in my halted liberation

Drew Walker

The Way You Love Me

I love the way you love me, love
I feel at ease
Comforted by your comfort
The way you seek to please

I wish I could offer you
That same certainty
My mind's confronting doubt
Indecision feeding off of me

Let me tell you, you're perfect
With all the dork and all your quirk
My feet are feeling restless, baby
If I go, will this still work?

I can't change my life for another
I've learned this lesson before
I can lead, but will you follow?
I wonder what's behind that door

Sometimes I need your spirit
When the feelings get too much
But you bury yourself deeply
When I just need a healing touch

There's an unwillingness to unleash
The you that's inside you
To be with me you must liberate
Yourself and all around you

I'm trying to see how I can adapt
To better fit your life
I'm spontaneous and unpredictable
It's not ideal in a wife

I walk a thin line
My destination is unknown
This life is but a process
In pursuit of feeling home

I cannot give things time
My life is not my future
I need to live for now
That's one thing I know for sure

And I love the way you love me, love
Amidst the chaos of my mind
Let me tell you that I love you, love
What a lucky love to find

Drew Walker

The End

I'm sorry if my messages are mixed
Love that exists can easily play tricks
Let me assure you that we really are done
The sound of reigniting doesn't sound one bit fun
We will never again be romantically together
No funny business, I've already cut the tether
I wish you the best from a great distance
But the door is closed, despite your persistence
One day I'm sure you'll see my face in passing
Let's walk on by, there's no time for rehashing
I hope you learned something on our journey shared
And know that in that time was the time I cared

Drew Walker

Sacred Soul

Breezy Bow River
Alberta blue skies
Sunscreen aromatics
Senses synthesize

The art within the artist
Is in the day to day
Intention in the energy
You took my breath away

Captivating spirit
I was on the other side
Your voice sang out to me
Filled my heart: a rising tide

Serenade the crowd
Can we feel the love from you?
It feels good, you want to share
And I felt it with you, too

                    Drew Walker

Apology

Do you think you've ever loved?
                    Truly loved
Where your entire being
                         Surrenders
To a world of unknown
Your body gives
Your mind bends
You build your life around feeling
Nothing matters except that love
And any barrier to it
Becomes abandoned

I think you were a barrier
To a love I truly believed
Now that love is gone
And I apologize

Drew Walker

Nightmares

You still haunt me in my dreams

And sometimes in my wake
The disrespect and ownership
Unconscious, stirring ache

When I try to self-express

I am met with breath-filled silence

You control your physicality

But enact emotional violence

What I really wanted

Was for you to truly see

All we ever were was equals

But below was always me

Drew Walker

Return

Every time I come back
I'm reminded of why I left
It's as if the choices I've made
Are a wrongdoing
My peace of mind, my liberation, my salvation:
An act of hatred

But I'll give myself to you
To prove that I am more than just your burden
To place my hand on the hearts of all
To answer your guilt-ridden call

When my life force is drained
I will no longer remain
Bound to a place with no feeling of home
Be grateful, for when I go remember:
Nobody owes anyone anything

Drew Walker

Dancer

I'm still waiting for that breakthrough
When I am fully with myself
Where you don't cross my mind every moment

I'll prance in femininity
I'll dance through divinity
An ethereal field flowing around me

But now, I grieve
In this house of sorrow
Replaying reminders
Imagining a life where it could work
It didn't work
It will never work

And I know
One day I will dance

Cosmic

I think of how we used to be.
Feeling you, feeling me
Connected in a way;   cosmically
Tell me that's what you still see

The only one that's felt this true
The one for me, the one for you
Frozen time, my heart's turned blue
Tell me, love, that you still do

I still want you every day
Lost control, to my dismay
Perhaps this moment was always our way
Tell me that you're here to stay

Drew Walker

In becoming something

I unbecame everything

Drew Walker

What If

Even as I'm falling in love
There's an underlying fear
Of temporary laws to nature
I envy others who can commit
To anything with a belief in permanence
I wish I could overcome my observations
And blindly, blissfully surrender
When I find myself in the moment
It isn't long before I drift
To the past, to the future
To the far corners of my mind
To the questions, potentials, what ifs
What if there was a way to coexist
Without being bound by certain confinement?
What if I get lost again?
What if these what ifs manifest destruction?
What if everything is perfect just the way it is?
But what if it isn't?

Drew Walker

Mouldy Mattress

You tell me it's time to get my mattress off the floor

For you, over here, there's an open door

You'll be lucky if you get a mattress at all

We joke, but surely it's a reasonable call

Who am I kidding; come into my bed

I haven't seen you in years, rest your head

I get caught in this dream; possible reality

But this daze may not be more than a fantasy

In person, you know, I have so much to say

But I can't bear the thought of scaring you away

So I go through the motions, play into what is near

Someday will be the day that I get to see you here

Drew Walker

Fungal State

My insides are made of love
And it's an overwhelming state of being
The energies around me
    have cracked my heart open
The beams pour out
    like sunlight between my fingertips:
Radiating, emanating
Last night I swam in the universe
    and we became one
Something that feels this good
    can never be wrong

Drew Walker

Love Addict

I saw you as the father of my children
While we were high on ecstasy
It took a love drug to get me there
To this intoxicating fantasy

The entire premise of us
Was bound to self implode
Parasitic symbiosis of energy:
You feeding off of my soul

I looked up the definition of manipulation
And was met with sinking clarity
Unscrupulous is my new favourite word
And you were clever to latch on to me

Drew Walker

Sometimes you have to break free

to be free

Drew Walker

Toxic Culture

Day in and day out
It's nine to five
The price you must pay
To stay alive
Backs may be breaking
But we're building wealth
A small toll may be taken:
Your well-being and health
They'll call to check in
You've already checked out
Rooted passions and values
You can do without
Use less, you're useless
This feels abusive
Flooding my mind
A disaster, intrusive
Seeing the signs,
You set boundaries
Shackled in the system
You'll never be free
Your lines will mean nothing
With repeated disrespect
Communicating inner limits
Yet somehow you've overstepped
Just when you're starting
To feel secure
A darkness clouds the room
And your heart is unsure
Not for a second
Should you have any power
Any thought of the sort
Welcomes devour
Inhale softly
I am breathing in life
Exhale slowly
I am met with strife

Feed off my goodness
This is the cost
Without a moral complex
I am feeling lost
This is the happenings
Of a spirit confined
Fitting in the box
That rich men designed

2/2

Drew Walker

Great Uncle

Catching up on our history
This family is a mystery
It's nearing time for a reunion
A confrontation, some communion

You tell me about hunting grouse
And how someday you'll sell your house
Pack up the car and hit the road
Live out your days where no one knows

We pause our talk to sing a song:
Unknown Legend by Neil Young

I wish the best for your neighbour's wife
And I'm glad you never lost your life
I show you the paint I dripped on the rug
And we feel together, a loving hug

Drew Walker

If I could choose to be anything

. I would be

Drew Walker

Boiling Point

There's a darkness within
It's boiling over
Coming up to the surface
Wish you could've been sober

Through it all I still feel
Wondrous light in my heart
It's a shame to feel it now
Only after we're apart

I cry into the air
At the thought of our attachment
The very thing that drew us close
And the source of my entrapment

I will always love you:
The words I hesitate to say
I worry, don't want to hurt you
But I'm the one that got away

You can thrive on your own:
I can't shake this feeling
But I need time to myself
And I need space for healing

Drew Walker

You're saying all the right things
I'm committed to your words
But promises lose value
When followed with inaction

Drew Walker

Perspective

Why compare yourself to me
When we exist so differently?
Strive to redirect that energy
To the you you used to be

Why compare myself to you
When we exist as a separate two?
That energy can be more true
When compared to the former Drew

Drew Walker

Spirit Quest

Frozen lashes and first kisses,
            we've got a good thing goin' on
I can picture a beautiful time with you
An everlasting evolution in our garden

I wonder if you've been
            to the garden before
Or if I will show you the way to the soul
To the beauty of incomprehensibility

Once we've arrived
            I will dig my feet into the soil
And when the ground feels balanced
            by your tender touch
I'll slowly allow them to take root

                        Drew Walker

The Black Lodge

Last night I was warmed
    by a room full of strangers

The cold air from outside

Couldn't get us inside

If it did, the collective burning of our hearts
    would be enough to heat an entire city

Immerse yourself in this energy

An experience of creativity

              Drew Walker

Ghost

A living ghost, I am haunted
In the thought of what once was
In the reality of my deception
In what I thought was called love

I was ready to give you my whole life
But you only wanted to take mine
I enabled a lowered standard
In my self-worth: gradual decline

I am healing, but I am haunted
Because your ghost still wants my mind
You want my thoughts, my inspiration
Most of all, you want my time

What are you to gain from reconnection?
Reaching out to share the burden
The burden of your rumination
Projecting on me your own stagnation

You still want to live in my mind
I'm not willing to give you the time
I can't do it anymore:
With no return, baring my soul

I feel I've been made a fool
Manipulated and treated cruel
Can't believe I was almost your wife
Now I'm blocking you from my life

I'll let you burn, I'll close the door
There's no need to tell you more
No obligation for explanation
I'm cutting off communication

Drew Walker

When I hit the bottom,

Did you see your reflection in me?

Drew Walker

Callum

You live your life

And I'll live mine

Support each others' dreams

Occasionally entwine

Never any pressure

I hope you're feeling fine

My door is always open

The path we walk: divine

This care that we feel

Doesn't need to be defined

Blessed by the stars

Brighter still, we shine

We should have a conversation

I'm toeing the line

My heart is ever grateful

For our beautiful design

Drew Walker

There is no formula

Just enjoy the process

Drew Walker

Love Connection

Meet me at the death place
I know you've been there too
The risk in love is pain
I'll always see it through

Love has many phases
Much to lose but more to gain
So when you say you want your freedom
Who am I to hold the chain?

It's impossible to predict
How this life will all unfold
Let's just help each other out
Give ourselves someone to hold

If a time ever comes
When we both feel a change
I'll kiss your heart and carry you
Bless the stars for this exchange

I'll think about you everyday
And wonder when our paths will cross
People flow in and out
Distance does not equate loss

When I see you again
I'll give a warm embrace
Meet new layers of your being
Feel your beauty and your grace

                    Drew Walker

People have different capacities for being

Drew Walker

Growth

There is nothing more powerful than nature:

Her ability to freeze time

To hold space in a way that is meaningful

May we all reflect nature in our endeavours

Dancing softly in the wind

Changing colours with the seasons

Creating beauty, even in decay

There's such wisdom in the simplicity

Of taking root with the intention to grow

Drew Walker

Closed Mind

Put me in a box
It'll organize your mind
Complicated sexuality
From a word: polyamory

What's there to judge
With an openness to love?
We're fighting with reality
Spectrums we choose not to see

If I could fit in there
It might ease your discomfort
But there's a missed opportunity
To embrace inclusivity

At the end of the day
There's no wrong way to exist
Accept another way to see
And respect my own desire to be free

Drew Walker

Tarnished

Today I received the most thoughtful gift
My entire body cried
Black tourmaline encased in silver
To carry your heart against mine

I can see you harvesting it from the river
Your frigid hand holding it
Protecting it
There's a piece of you in this gift
Yet my gratitude is only articulated in a question:

Do you really think that love is enough?

Still I wear this necklace
I wear it with pride
A symbol of the most paralyzing love
And two hearts that travel together,
Apart

Drew Walker

Process

I don't want to fit in the lines
For my spirit in this moment shines
I'm perfecting imperfection
Room to grow, to set intention
Accepting faults and defects
Inner wisdom: my soul protects
Life is an evolving process
With many meanings for success

Drew Walker

Maggie

The embodiment of love

Ours souls are feeling true

Looking deep within my heart

And staring back is you

Drew Walker

Devotion

You make me want to start traditions
Be around for all editions
To be myself: you give permission
My true love, without condition
I will not manifest opposition
Our feelings surely will transition
The love will carry; our shared mission
"Our paths align," says my intuition
I hold no fears or suspicions
Taking joy in this composition
Magic aura, contagious emissions
I bow to you in complete submission
I knew you'd come: a premonition
Heartache gone into remission
For you I have a proposition:
Let's embark on an expedition
There'll be no lack of recognition
We'll reach new heights in coalition
A theoretical inquisition
Has now become a new addition

Drew Walker

Acatenango

Guatemala hiking
Up the side of a volcano
Step by step we ascend
To reach the fire: Fuego

My body has its limits
My mind says it's unsure
To add another summit here:
My unnecessary cure

You see, hiking is quite challenging
As I build strength in little legs
Experience the positivity
So I will welcome future crags

I'm well above the clouds
I'll take it in my stride
In the distance it's erupting
So I watch the lava slide

Impressed with my ability
I am filled with gratitude
Perfection in this earthly world
In what this body, here, can do

Fireworks coming from her mouth
Smoke as she exhales
A glowing landslide from afar
Nature always prevails

Drew Walker

Oceans

I'll cross oceans to be with you
I'm beginning to see
The little pieces of me
Why try and seek to make that complete?
Wherever I go
I may never be whole
That's a beautiful tragedy
And you feel like home

Drew Walker

When everything becomes too much,

That's when you're supposed to cry

Drew Walker

Those Words

I don't want to say I love you
Because the words hold so much meaning
I think restraint is best
But the truth: it's all I'm feeling

I don't want to use it lightly
For it may lose its significance
But I can't seem to find another word
For your effervescent radiance

How could I possibly
Say it any other way
This feeling pouring out
I must express and not delay

To hear and say those words so much
Tired, we may grow
So we'll make new words and learn new languages
Know our love will always show

Drew Walker

Man at Sea

Can anyone see
        out in the sea
That thing over there
        or is it just me?

To stay above water
        my mind has gone under
A creature of land
        confined, filled with wonder

What's the point anymore?
        Will I ever find my way to shore?
Instinct's taken over me
        To never be what was before

Free amongst this open place
        My sanity has been erased
This loneliness will overtake
        Another thought I must replace

Drew Walker

Villi

If heaven is a place on Earth
I've found it here with you
Glistening, gleaming, glowing
The sunlight kisses our skin
Winter sheds its layers
Seasonal rebirth: dripping into Spring
Soaking up moments
Loving, holding, breathing, feeling

Drew Walker

Insight

Maybe we can all feel everything
But we've trained ourselves to limit perception
A coping mechanism, perhaps.

For how could a person go about their day
When they are struck with sheer awe
            at the beauty of existence
        and the reality of its impermanence
All in one moment: collective overwhelm.

Drew Walker

Motions

I feel my feelings fading

Not in a way that is negative

Merely an observation

My body is coping with living

Out of necessity instead of being

As I transition from human:

Open, wild, free

To human:

Busy, structured, paid

My body has decided that,

In order to protect me from reality

It's better to feel nothing at all

Drew Walker

Please Divinity

I don't want to say I'm lonely
But I want for you to hold me
Wrap your arms around me tight
A warm embrace into the night
It's not that I'm feeling empty at all
My heart is full, to share is my call
This beauty and love, it overflows
A feeling of freedom that few people know

But your heart is not free
I'm learning to accept what will be
I trust that the Earth will bring what I need
On this journey of life as we all grow from seed
In every moment I'll be present
I'm finding now to be quite pleasant
So I'll continue to let this all unfold
Divine timing will lead us all to gold

Now is the time to feel what I'm feeling
Later I will feel what this life will be revealing

Drew Walker

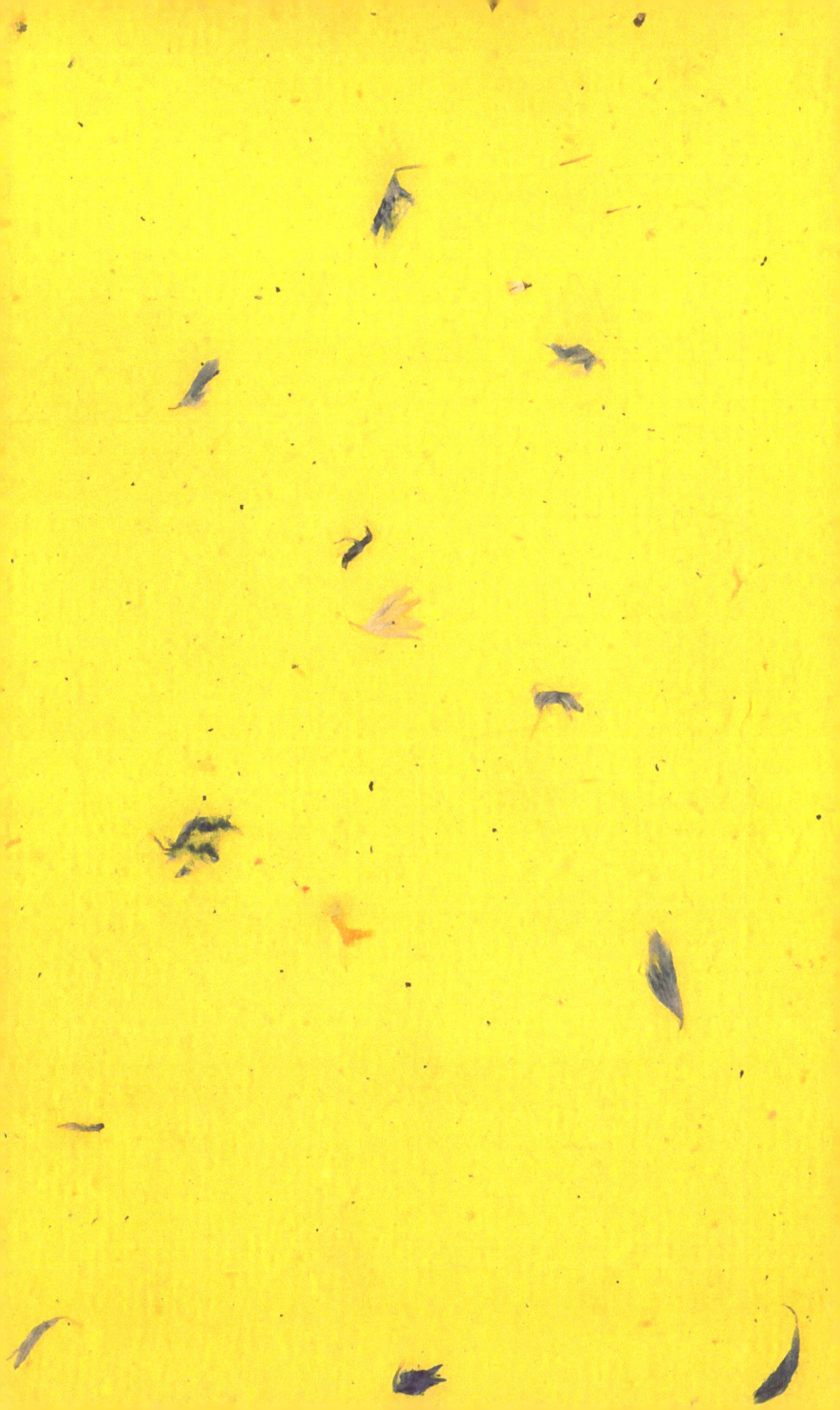

Hopeful

Falling in love with you all over
I've been dimming in my light
Let us run into the forest
And feel our passion reignite

You see, I've been feeling so busy
With my duties everyday
The city noise is overstimulating
Here with you, I'm here to stay

Losing track of time
As we're so caught up in the moment
I was busy overthinking
But right now the world is silent

You're a beautiful reflection
Another person filled with love
Could it be I'm finally ready?
To be enamored of

Drew Walker

In Your Dreams

You've been dreaming of me
Of a light, easy love
My hair wisps smoothly
As rays of sunlight find their way through
Gently, golden strands, flowing
A soft comfort overcomes you
When I look into your eyes
A knowing
That it's more than just a look
An understanding, appreciation
Of a shared existence
Even if only in dreams
This love pours into my wake
It does not dull with the passing of time
My heart has softened, delicately beating
Hope - of a life alongside you
Wonder - in the potential of a love that's true
Physically, we couldn't be further away
Spiritually, I feel you every second, every day
Escape with me behind your eyes while you sleep
In this dream world, you're the company I keep

Drew Walker

Onion

Boy you've got it all
I just want to sit inside
Peel back your layers
And take you for a ride
Go deeper than the surface
Feel your true heart
Reveal inner being
Go slowly at the start
Why rush a good thing
When there's no end in sight
Connection in energy
Sends love into flight
I've learned before:
Moving fast is not adept
Instant gratification:
A form of disrespect
So let's just take our time
Build a strong foundation
Get to know each other first
And embrace this sensation

Drew Walker

You stunting my growth

Is what helped me grow the most

Drew Walker

Multiple Lovers

Until I see you again
I am utterly confused
What will be between us,
My dear muse?
I can't break this wall down
Until I get some closure
I'm at a standstill
But must keep my composure
How easy it would be
If our hearts moved on
Years continue passing
Your presence remains strong
I'm trying to let go
I'm investing in new lovers
It hardly feels fair
With lingered feelings for another
I suppose it's ethical
As my truth is in the open
My love has become boundless
When I share it all with him
But I know that nothing is permanent
I know it all will change
I think it'd break my heart
For any lover to estrange
What would break it even more
Is carrying this grief
Overthinking this predicament
Would be my love's thief
I must let this love grow
Overflow on my surrounds
Maybe it'll travel
Through the earth, without bounds

Drew Walker

Smitten

I am feeling seen for the first time
Synchronized through our eyes
Free from fear of demise

I am feeling heard for the first time
Speaking clear, ear to ear
The words we share are truth, sincere

I am feeling held for the first time
Bodies from within, skin to skin
It's a simple ease to let you in

I am feeling loved for the first time
In a healthy way, a fine display
No doubts at all, we're here to stay

Drew Walker

A disorganized mind

Makes a disorganized reality

But who's to say what's real anyways?

Drew Walker

Winter Solstice

Today the shadows take their course
As they convene together at once
Winter air permeates my bones
Darkness has come; she confronts

These months leading up
Have been a true test
My loneliest heartache;
This feeling can rest

It's time to let go
I'm coming to know this
The days will be lighter
December Solstice

Drew Walker

Functional family: a true oxymoron

Drew Walker

Spirit

Hey you, I know you're in there
I've found my way here
Traveled a great distance
To get to you my dear
Show me what you're made of
The language that you speak
Seeping through his skin
You can make me feel complete
At home
When you reveal inner light
Flowing softly through the air
Hold me close into the night
I'm looking in to his eyes
And I feel closer to you
Let's get lost, get higher
Get to know that this is true
I'm not living on a timeline
But in an unfolding dream
The director of my lifetime
You're becoming a main theme

Drew Walker

If I love you

   Will I lose myself?

               Drew Walker

No Love

When I think of you
I feel a weight in my chest
A tumultuous heaviness
Of my own buried knowing

A knowing that I wish not to know
About a feeling that I wish to feel

I long for freedom
Liberation in my being
Love flows in presence
In alignment with my senses

All this time you've wanted more time
I wish we used our time right,
                        at the right time

Drew Walker

I liked your dog more than I liked you

Drew Walker

His Eyes

I can'T remember the look in your eyes
What are you without the memory?
A single tear falls down my cheek
Distance from the arms that held me
I feel happy for you, living your life
Maybe it's called compersion
Something's not right, I hear in your voice
The you I know is another version
This soul of mine is patient
For this love I'll wait all time
But there's no proper affirmation
That you'll share your heart with mine
I'm not asking for your life
For your service or security
I'm asking for an experience
Of a higher love that's true and free
When you're here I'll know you're ready
To accept this love that is
And I'll reform all those memories
Of the eyes I'm lost in, his.

Drew Walker

One Year

One year of loving you
And I'm feeling so much better
One year of living true
From the way that you have led her

Being with you there are no walls
I'm basking in reality
When away my heart it calls
For the arms that hold me

Committed to you, I'm completely free
Mental hurdles I'm getting over
The kindest hearts as we just be
I am honoured to be your lover

I trust you more than with my life
It feels like we're family
I wonder if I'll be your wife
Not one for marriage, but we'll see

My favourite part: your inner child
To you, I can not lie
Let your spirit runneth wild
This love can never die

Drew Walker

There are no trees that are not cool

Drew Walker

Best Friends

We all have many soulmates
If it's meant to be, we'll collide
Time and time we've found each other
Drinking tea, fireside

There's a beautiful nostalgia
At the thought of time passed
This love transcends our lifetime
A connection built to last

Nothing here is permanent
Next time we meet won't be the same
Devoted evolution
Our present spirits will remain

I feel truly honoured
To have a friend in you
We laugh all night until we cry
Authentic, pure, and true

Drew Walker

Nature's Cycle

I like to think of death
as speckles of light
A passing of the body;
end of physical life
Like sparks from a fire
rising up in the night
Tilt your head up:
they become stars shining bright

It's like a rising from the ashes
into everything around
It's a dispersion of our energy
can you feel it's surround?
It's connected to the air,
to our hearts and to the ground
When I really think about it,
it's truly quite profound

A great source of challenge
is putting my finger on It
The right words don't exist:
language as a limit
Mirrored cycles on this earth
guide my mind to submit
- No impossibility in our ability
to eternally transmit

Drew Walker

Gratitude

To the Edmonton Public Library for maintaining their printers and scanners. To Janice Laud, for making the most beautiful paper I've ever laid eyes on. To the team at Wild Skies Press, for supporting my poetry professionally. To my community of friends, family, and supporters for your patience and love. To the earth, for providing me with the space and pace to be creative. To the readers, thank you for reading and feeling with me.

My final message: strive to do what is right in all moments given all the information at hand.

Love and light,

Drew Walker

Drew Walker

About the Author:

Born and raised in Edmonton, Canada, Drew
Walker has spent her young adulthood striving
to obtain wealth in experiences. International
travel, deep connection to nature, and the
navigation of complex relationships inspire
her poetry. Outside of her writing, Walker
is a professional landscape designer,
beekeeper, and community steward. Walker's
poems offer a glimpse into her personal
journals in which she shares honest
contemplations, unexpressed feelings, and
messages to lovers past.

Since the release of her debut collection,
Confines of a free Spirit (2020), Walker
has performed at several spoken word events.
She is also the creator of Real Talker with
Drew Walker, a podcast which features an
inside look at the stories and inspiration
behind her poems.

Other Books from Wild Skies Press

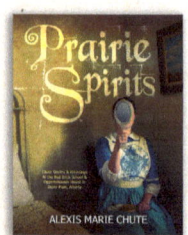

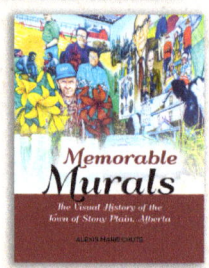

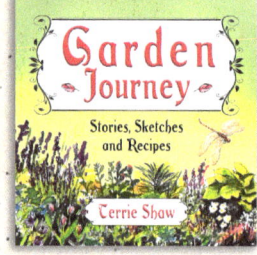

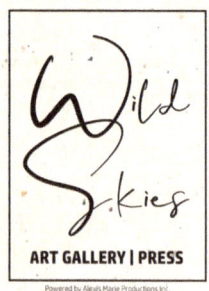

Wild Skies
ART GALLERY | PRESS
Powered by Alexis Marie Productions Inc.

www.WildSkiesPress.com